EMP⊘WER

THE PASSION WITHIN

RISE FROM THE COMFORT OF
THE ORDINARY!

BY TERRI DADE

Copyright Notice

Copyright © 2011

ISBN 978-0-9832154-0-0

FIRST EDITION

Cover design and Layout by Maier Tudor

TABLE OF CONTENTS

ACKNOWLEGMENTS to Friends and Family

To my husband, thank you for your patience throughout the book project. You have been by my side until I produced a finished product.

To my sister Jennifer, thanks for your continued support. I owe so much. I thank you for helping me to find myself and to grow spiritually. Ironically, I have learned so much from my little sister. You have been a perfect example of what a lady should be like.

To my sisters Toni, Lynne, Sharone, Rochelle, Tammy, Cheryl, Juanita, and Lisa, thank you for your friendship and your support. I also thank my aunt, Brenda Sabree, an established author who encouraged me to continue to write. To my sister Maria Reams, thanks for reading the book and for the incredible work that you did on my web site.

Thanks also to Kim Daniels and Yolanda Pikemuccini (my author sisters) for inspiring me; to Herb, for your friendship and support; to Rhynell for your friendship and support, and for all your help with the book—your feedback, and the amazing job with the video for the web site. To all of you, I could not have written this book without your love and support.

ACKNOWLEGMENT to the Reader

Thank you for taking the time out of your busy schedule to read and enjoy this book. Certainly I am forever grateful for your support. It is my sincere hope that you are able to take something from this message that will help to motivate and uplift you to your greater self, and that you are able to share this with others.

CHAPTER 1

What Is Passion?

D o you have a desire deep inside you to fulfill a dream and live a life filled with enthusiasm? Perhaps you haven't quite found the passion that creates that kind of life. That's okay. Passion isn't always obvious; it can sometimes lie below the surface, hidden under other experiences.

In fact, passion can be like the juicy flesh of a peach, which is buried under the skin—which is covered with less-than-appetizing fuzz. But when you peel the skin away or bite right through it, you taste the wonderful flavor of the fruit and experience the delicious juice dripping down your chin, and you get lost in the pure pleasure of eating that wonderful piece of fruit.

Passion can be like that. It might be an ordinary day (with a little fuzz of monotony, like the outside of a peach) when all of a sudden you have a new thought or try a new activity or read about something that you aren't familiar with—and there it is, that feeling that comes from your core and lets you know that this is no ordinary thought, experience, or discovery…it is something that resonates through your very being. That, my friend, is passion!

Tiger Woods found his passion at the age of one, when a golf club was put in his hands for the first time.[1] Even at a young age, his skills were exceptional and his interest was high. Tiger was fortunate to have a father who not only recognized his interest and skill, but was willing to put the necessary time and energy into helping his young son develop his potential. According to his biography on Starpulse.com, "Tiger's skills were so good at such a young age that it landed him an appearance on the Mike Douglas Show in 1978. The two-year-old Woods' appearance put him up against the legendary comedian Bob Hope in a putting contest."[1] And Tiger was only three years old when "he shot a 48 over nine holes at one of his hometown courses." And the rest, as they say, is history.

In 1896, when Harlan Sanders was six years old, he was forced into a responsible role when his father died and his mother had to enter the workforce. Young Harlan began doing much of the family's cooking, and within a year he had already mastered several regional dishes.[2] Young Harlan had found his passion, but the time was apparently not right for his passion to fully blossom, because he spent the next thirty years working jobs ranging from streetcar conductor to insurance salesman. When he was forty, Sanders—who was then operating a service station—started cooking for travelers. By 1935 he was recognized by the Governor of Kentucky for his "contribution to the state's cuisine," and in 1955 he began a franchise business with Kentucky Fried Chicken. At the age of seventy-four, Colonel Sanders sold his interest in the business for two million dollars.

Harlan Sanders never let go of his passion. He kept cooking and experimenting, even while he had to work other jobs to support himself and his family. And that's the most important thing to understand about passion: it may find you at a young age and blossom into full purpose almost immediately...or it may take twenty, forty, or even sixty more years for it to come to full bloom.

I was very young when I discovered my passion for being an entrepreneur and owning my own business. When I was ten years old, my friend Jeanette (who always had great ideas) and I decided that we were going to start a business. We made a decision to come up with a product and sell it. It was that simple! Our young minds searched for possibilities. We found stuffed animals that we no longer enjoyed playing with and a pretty plastic container that at one time had held a perfume bottle. We selected a stuffed animal that fit nicely into the case, tied it up with a ribbon, and lo and behold! We had a product ready to sell.

Youth was probably on our side; after all, who doesn't appreciate a young entrepreneur filled with passion and excitement? Our first stop was the grandmother of another childhood friend, and we made the sale. What an accomplishment! We were entrepreneurs! Our self-esteem, confidence, and entrepreneurial spirits sky-rocketed!

And my entrepreneurial spirit is still alive. Although I have worked in a government job for thirty years, I am still filled with the passion to move forward with a business of my own, one that will help people, whether they are just starting out in life or have lived for many years, to find their own passion and purpose.

In the last few years, I've discovered what a difference having a passion for something can make in our lives... and I wish I had discovered it when I was in my teens instead of in my forties. And that's part of my passion: to bring the possibilities, excitement, and enthusiasm about life to people who think they are too young to know their passion and people who think they are too old to follow it, and to everyone in between. That's the purpose of this book, to pump you up and get you excited about life and its possibilities, whether you are fifteen or eighty-five—or even younger or older!

Passion takes different forms for different people. For some of us, passion is a quiet love, a desire that keeps moving forward in our lives no matter what else may be going on. Colonel Sanders is a perfect example of that. He loved to cook, and throughout his life, despite having a huge responsibility thrust on him at a young age, he continued to follow his passion. And behind his passion was a purpose—to combine his love for food with business.

If there is no passion in your life,
then have you really lived?
Find your passion, whatever it may be.
Become it, and let it become you, and you will find
great things happen FOR you, TO you,
and BECAUSE of you.
~T. Alan Armstrong

When we are living our passion, other strong emotions surface that help us overcome any obstacles that might cross our path. Living our passion continuously 'pushes the envelope' of our conception of what is "normal." The famous artist Pablo Picasso is a good example of this. At a young age he showed an interest in and a talent for art. Because his father was a professor at the School of Arts and Crafts in Malaga, Spain, Picasso began to study at the Academy of Arts in Madrid.[3] He exhibited his first works at the age of thirteen, but because he was an innovator and didn't want to be bound by the artistic ideas and interpretations of others, he stepped away from a formal education in art and moved to Paris. Throughout his long life, Picasso remained true to his passion and his ideas of what art is and should be.

Picasso was willing to take risks and be true to his own ideas; he wasn't bound by the opinions of others. And that's passion! People who are consumed with passion dance to the beat of their own drummer. Passion is filled with audacity, fearlessness, and spunk. And passion changes, evolving into what it was meant to be and changing the person who is true to their passion. Picasso again is a great example. If you look at the over 250,000 works of art Picasso created in his lifetime[4] you will see myriad styles, and concepts. He continually changed, and his art changed with him, but his dedication to his art—however it looked at any given time—always stayed strong. *That* is passion!

Truly living your own passion means that you are willing to step out, be different, and go beyond the confines of what is expected. Passionate people take risks! One of the first prerequisites for living your passion and accomplishing your dreams is to be willing to go outside your comfort zone, trusting that the strong emotions and beliefs inside you will guide you and lead you to accomplish that which you were born to do. Just imagine all the amazing works of art that our world would be missing if Picasso had stayed within the confines of the Academy of Art in Spain! He would still have been a good artist, but would he have been the amazing, world-famous artist that he became? Would his fame have endured even thirty-seven years after his death? I rather doubt it. I believe that his passion, his desire to be who he was and create what he was passionate about, is what developed his greatness.

As I approach retirement from my government job, I'm beginning to think more and more about my passion and what I'm going to do with it. And in contemplating these thoughts, I discovered something really exciting. One day, my husband and I were just shooting the breeze, and I asked him what he was passionate about. He had to think about it for a minute, but when he told me what it was I was shocked and delighted to find that we both have the same passion. Our vision is to touch as many people as we can, especially focusing on young people. Now just imagine two forces that are one with God, having the same vision…nothing but powerful!

Do you have greatness inside you? It doesn't matter if you are thirteen, thirty, or one-hundred-and-three. If greatness is there, and if it is backed by a passionate desire to live that greatness and release your talent, creativity, and intelligence into the world, you can do it!

Since you are reading this book, you too must have a passion. Or perhaps you have a driving desire to find your passion. Whichever it is for you, this book has been written to help you understand what passion is, how to find yours (if you haven't already), what to do once you do find it, and how to reach your full potential.

Living your passion is all about experiencing every step of the journey. If you want an uncomplicated life that is bereft of emotions, experiences and adventures, then you probably should put this book down and forget about finding or following your passion. A life that is dedicated to following a passion is innately filled with emotions, complications, experiences, and adventures.

Some people automatically equate following their passion with making millions of dollars, but that's not always the case. Mother Teresa had a passion to serve God and help people. She didn't become rich, but she changed the lives of people all over the world. Don't deceive yourself that having a passion has to be about making a pile of money, although those two things do sometimes coincide. And having a lot of money doesn't necessarily bring happiness or contentment—many celebrities are perfect examples of that. But following your passion can and does bring happiness and contentment.

Martin Luther King, Mahatma Gandhi, and Nelson Mandela all had a passion for equality, and they were willing to endure many hardships in order to follow the paths on which their passions had set them. They each changed the lives of millions of people, but their passions didn't bring them riches. Oprah Winfrey, on the other hand, has a passion for helping others and making positive changes in the world, and her passions have led her to wealth.

What about you? Do you want to change the world or do you want to get rich? Do you want to affect the lives of people in your community or the lives of people all over the globe? Do you want to experience the wonder of writing a novel, creating a painting, or sculpting a work of art and selling it to a small audience of people within your community? Or do you want to create a masterpiece that becomes known and recognized throughout the world? Would you rather quietly teach a classroom of children and know you are making a difference in their lives, or speak in front of audiences of thousands and bring a new way of thinking or being into their consciousness?

Everyone's passion is unique. If you are trying to mold or control your passion, you are stifling it. Passion has a mind and a soul of its own. To truly live your passion, you have to be willing to give up control and take the wild roller-coaster ride that living your passion requires.

For some people, that is too high a price to pay. For others, the consequences of not following their passion are unbearable. The regret of lost dreams and the apathy toward life that comes from pushing one's passion into deep, dark chasms of fear and conformity are an unthinkable way to live.

What about you? Are you ready to discover, live, enjoy, dream, believe, and master your passion? Good! Then you've come to the right place. Take a deep breath and together we'll take the steps that will lead you to living out your full potential!

CHAPTER 2

Finding Your Passion

The seed of passion is sometimes planted by the things you do, the people you meet, the places you travel to, and even the movies you see or the books you read. Without those experiences you might not find the passion that is deep within you. Can a person who sits quietly in a room their entire lifetime find passion? Perhaps, but it's unlikely. It is the experience of life that triggers passion, and it is the living of life that brings passion to a full explosion.

Maybe you've already found your passion. Perhaps you know that you come alive when you stand in front of an audience to give a speech. Or perhaps the time you spend working in your garden is sweeter than any other moment in your day. Or maybe just the thought of having your own business and being able to run it on a daily basis instead of working for someone else makes your heart beat a little faster.

Many people discover their passion while they are still in high school. Singer/songwriter Taylor Swift[5], who began writing songs at the age of five, signed a record deal with RCA Records at the age of thirteen and began winning awards for her singing at the age of seventeen. Taylor demonstrates perfectly that age is not a determining factor when it comes to discovering or living your passion. So don't let being young stop you; Tiger Woods was one year old and Taylor Swift was five when it all began for them.

Or perhaps you are retired or about to retire (like I am) and you know that it's time to pursue something you really love doing, but you have spent so much of your life concerned about providing a living for your family that you don't think you have a clue about what your passion is. Listen to your heart and pay attention to where it leads you. For instance, if you are thinking enough about finding your passion that you've picked up this book...your time has come. Something inside you is pushing you and yelling at you: "Find me!...it's time to find me."

There is no greatness without a passion to be great, whether it's the aspiration of an athlete or an artist, a scientist, a parent, or a businessperson.

~Anthony Robbins

Something to keep in mind, however, is that passion is not an 'on-demand' kind of experience. You may find it young and then spend many years doing something you like and enjoy but are not passionate about. And then one day you have an experience, or a thought... and there it is—that feeling deep in your gut that lets you know that this thought or experience is somehow different. When that happens, passion is poking its way out of the shadows to become a force in your life.

I know that most books on passion tell you to make lists of what you love to do, and those tactics work because they focus you on the things you love. But in reality, passion usually shows up when you allow yourself to freely think the thoughts that appear in your mind and experience the things that interest you. If Taylor Swift hadn't begun writing at the age of five when the words and music started manifesting in her mind, she might not have discovered the passion that was deep within her soul, and the world would be without a lot of wonderful music. If Picasso had not paid attention to his disinterest in drawing, painting, or sculpting like everyone else, his passion for creating unique art might not have been ignited.

So, yes, make lists and ask yourself questions like:

o   What are five things I really enjoy doing?

o   What would I willingly do for free if given the opportunity?

o   What are some of the things I do that others often comment positively about?

o   What traits do I love about myself?

o   If I won the lottery, what would I spend my life doing?

o   What makes me smile?

o   What are five things I'm really good at?

o   What would I regret not doing?

o   If I were put in a room all by myself and could choose to do anything, what would it be?

o   When I was a child, what dreams or ideas did I have?

o   What am I envious of when I see others doing it?

o   Do I have a secret desire deep within my heart to do or accomplish something that I have never told anyone about?

Let yourself make lists of things you love to do, and just keep making lists until all your thoughts are down on paper. But don't stop there.

Spend some time in the library or in a bookstore. What kinds of books interest you? What section do you head towards: fiction or non-fiction? Is there one particular book that jumps off the shelf at you? Follow your instincts and go with the flow…you never know where your passion might be hiding!

Or look to outside sources to help you unearth your passion, dreams, and visions. In her book, The Artist's Way: A Spiritual Path to Higher Creativity, Julia Cameron provides a twelve-week process for opening up your curiosity and helping you find inspiration.

Or try using visualization to open your mind to all possibilities. Visualizing is simply clearing a space in your mind for thoughts and ideas to surface in the form of pictures or scenes that play out like a movie. Begin the whole process by going to a quiet space and just sitting in a relaxed position. Ask yourself: What is my passion? Why am I here on this earth? What am I meant to do? And then just let your mind wander. Don't censor it. Don't stop the thoughts, pictures, and visualizations from coming. And whatever you do, don't judge them. Just let your mind stroll among the possibilities the way you would meander through a field of wild flowers, stopping sometimes to closely examine one or enjoy its beauty, but not judging or looking for the most beautiful flower in the field, simply walking among all the possibilities until you find one you can't resist.

If you are unfamiliar with visualizations, there are many CDs and Web sites devoted to guided visualizations that you can listen to while you sit quietly with your eyes closed. A friend of mine has a favorite guided visualization that she often uses to help herself stay connected with her passion and purpose. The link to it is *http://www.andreahess.com/freemini_processor.asp*

Click on "free download" and you will be connected with a forty-five minute guided visualization specifically for finding your passion and purpose.

And if these methods don't bring you something that makes you jump up and down and yell with joy... that's okay too. Remember, sometimes you don't find your passion; sometimes it finds you. So live each day open to the possibility of life and something wonderful happening in your life. It could happen today or tomorrow, or it could happen when you're eighty. That doesn't mean that life up until that moment wasn't good or wonderful. Remember, being happy is a choice; it doesn't happen by fate or by accident.

So live, love, enjoy, explore, experience, be curious, be open, be non-judgmental…and always be ready and willing to find and live your passion! Because only with an inquisitive mind will you will find your true passion.

But don't expect that your passion will be something that you are innately good at, because that's not always the case. But it will be something that you really enjoy doing, something you don't want to stop doing, something you are willing to put time and effort into learning and becoming better at.

As professional skateboarder Tony Hawk[6] says, "I never stopped riding my skateboard and never stopped progressing as a skater. There have been many, many times when I've been frustrated because I can't land a maneuver. I've come to realize that the only way to master something is to keep at it—despite the bloody knees, despite the twisted ankles, despite the mocking crowds."

So don't set up the impossible expectation that your passion will be something at which you will immediately excel. Even Tiger Woods has had to practice, practice, practice to keep at the top of his game. And the songs that Taylor Swift now writes are quite different from the ones she wrote at the age of five. When you have a desire to do something again and again, no matter the challenge or difficulties…that's passion. When you can't stop thinking about an experience or an idea, and all you want to do is talk about it to anybody who will listen (and some who try not to)…that's passion.

Let go of the preconception that finding your passion will make your life easier. It's not true. As I said earlier in this book, passion will push the envelope in your life—expecting more, demanding more, requiring more. Mother Teresa's passion for helping people around the world did not bring ease and comfort to her life, but it brought satisfaction, contentment, and happiness. Maybe not the kind of happiness many of us would seek, but happiness that was ideal for her. And that's passion!

Sometimes living your passion is about giving your life totally to what you believe in. Again, I use the examples of Mother Teresa, Martin Luther King, and Nelson Mandela. They all dedicated their lives to doing what they were passionate about…what they truly believed in. Mother Teresa lived in poverty, Nelson Mandela spent many years in prison, and Martin Luther King died at a young age, but if we were able to ask any of them if they would do it all again, I believe that they would all answer with a resounding, "Yes!"

You may have to ignore the opinions of others when you pursue your passion, because if you get stuck on what other people think, you might miss finding what you are on this earth to do. I'm sure when Bill Gates discovered his love of computers when he was in the seventh grade,[7] he was probably looked upon as a bit of a geek. But isn't it fortunate for all of us that he didn't let that stop him? I wouldn't be sitting here at my personal computer typing this book if Mr. Gates had not followed his passion because it wasn't the "cool" thing to do!

Andrea Bocelli, who began piano lessons at the age of six, did not find and follow his passion for singing opera until he was thirty-four,[8] a point in his life that some "experts" said was too late to begin. Bocelli ignored the critics and has now been singing opera for close to twenty years. Aren't we glad that he didn't listen to those who tried to discourage him?

Passion often requires persistence. English author Mary Wesley published her first children's book at the age of fifty-seven, and she was seventy-one years old when she published her first adult fiction. She continued writing, and several of her books were turned into television series or movies in the 1980s and 1990s. Ms. Wesley stopped writing at the age of eighty-four, saying simply, "If you haven't got anything to say, don't say it."[9]

Well-known chef Julia Child was thirty-six when she attended the Cordon Bleu cooking school in Paris, and she was forty-nine when she published her famous cookbook, Mastering the Art of French Cooking.[10]

The point is that you are never too young or too old to begin living your passion, and if you're reading this book, something has triggered that interest in you. Either you have a passion that is trying to get your attention, or you are a person who does not want to live life as it "should be," but wants to live life to the fullest, the way it "can be." Whatever the case may be, your passion is waiting for you to discover it—or for you to be open to it discovering you! And it doesn't matter how many different jobs or experiences you have had, or how many years you live before you do. Given the opportunity, your passion will arrive in your life when it is supposed to.

As I mentioned at the beginning of this book, my husband and I share a passion for touching and making a difference in as many lives as we can. And we have a real passion for touching the lives of young people, letting them know that anything truly is possible. We're starting with this book, opening up the thought process and emphasizing that you are never too young or too old to find and live your passion. So we've begun. We don't know where this will take us or how living our passion will play out, we just know that we are on the path.

What about you? Have you already discovered your passion, but you're not sure what to do now that you have? Or are you still making excuses for why you can't live your passion? Or are you filled with fear, listening to a voice that says, "Who do I think I am that…"

That's okay. All the things I mentioned above (and many more) are about the process of finding and living our passion. Wherever you are is okay. However you are feeling at this very moment is okay. Your thoughts, your journey, your passion, and the results of living your passion will be absolutely unique to you. Think of living your passion as working with clay: you have an idea of what you want it to look like when you're done, but many factors will go into developing the finished project—the clay itself, the humidity of the particular day, and even your hands which are more nimble some days than others. True artists understand that the artistic process often has a mind of its own. If you talk to people who write fiction, many will tell you that the characters in their books or stories, "take on a mind of their own." Discovering and living your passion is much like that: it will look the way it is meant to look.

And don't hesitate to ask God or your Higher Power for help or guidance. There is a spirit and connection that resides in every one of us that links us to something much bigger than ourselves. Some of us believe we have a destiny and a purpose in this lifetime…if that is your belief, engage in activities such as prayer and meditation that can help you discover that purpose or destiny. And then be willing to listen and have the courage to take the steps you need to take to get on the path outlined for you. Live each moment to the fullest and be open to the possibilities. It's exciting. It's fun!

So begin! Start the journey of finding and living your passion—whatever is true for you right at this very moment.

CHAPTER 3

What to do once You find It

Passion is as individual and unique as we are. Two people can have passion for the same thing, but they will experience it and play it out differently. For instance, Martin Luther King, Mahatma Ghandi, and Nelson Mandela all had a passion for freedom and equality, but they acted on that passion in different ways—ways that were unique to who they were.

And your passion will be the same way for you. Just because you may have a passion for starting an Internet business doesn't mean your business will look, feel, or function like other businesses on the Internet. Perhaps you have a passion for singing. The way you sing, the songs you want to sing, and your interpretation of those songs will be uniquely yours. Just think of the thousands of singers who have CDs available today; no two are exactly alike.

You may have a passion for making a difference in this lifetime, and you may do it by helping one person at a time, or you may do something that affects a large group of people, or even the world. My husband and I have a passion for positively influencing young people, beginning with those in our community, but hopefully expanding out into the world.

What you do with your passion is up to you. You get to be at the reins and create what you want from something you love. Some people have a passion for discovering new things. Others want to explore a talent or bring new dimensions to something that already exists (as Picasso did with art). Wherever your passion lies, it will take persistence and dedication to bring it into full bloom and create whatever it is you want to create. Moving forward with passion also takes courage, because passion often takes us beyond the bounds of what has already been done. Most of the greatest inventions in the world have been created because of someone's passion.

Bill Gates admits to "loving new things and solving problems" for as long as he can remember. "So when I sat down at a computer for the first time in seventh grade, I was hooked."[7] And when Gates and Paul Allen started Microsoft in the 1970s, they not only had a passion for what they were doing, they had a vision of "a computer on every desk and in every home."

Remember, this was at a time when computers were the size of refrigerators. But Gates and Allen didn't let the reality of what then existed get in the way of what they believed could be and what they wanted to do. And because of their passion and their vision, personal computers are a part of everyday life for the majority of us, and they've helped change the way we live and do business.

When work, commitment, and pleasure all become one
And you reach that deep well where passion lives,
Nothing is impossible.
~Author Unknown

I have always made it a point to surround myself with positive people and individuals who share my passion for life. My mentor, Herb Manley, became very successful in the real estate market and built an empire. But he didn't become successful overnight.

Herb worked twelve-hour shifts and even worked on his days off until he made a substantial amount of money—enough for a down-payment and the closing costs—to purchase his first home. He then made repairs to that home and rented it out. He repeated this process ten times over until he accumulated over ten homes and an apartment building. It took him ten years to get to where he is now. And Herb says it wasn't as easy as it sounds; he had some bumps and bruises along the way. But anyone can do this. It takes time, patience, and a willingness to succeed.

Although Herb has become very successful in real estate, it is not his passion. His passion is helping people purchase their first home. He gets a good feeling inside when he helps someone through the process, and when the person he helped calls him the day after settlement, telling him that they are now a homeowner. I am happy to say that I am one of his students and that he helped me purchase my first rental property. So Hetb is now living his passion.

Perhaps you are young. Perhaps you are still in high school and know that you want to move forward with your life, doing something that really makes a difference to you. Maybe you love art and everyone is telling you that you can't make a living as an artist. Well…if you want to live your passion, you'll figure out a way to make a living as an artist. Just because it hasn't been done doesn't mean it can't be.

When I was forty-six years old, the desires of my heart started to surface. It was like all the pieces started to fall into place, and the puzzle of my life began to form a picture of what life could and would look like. It was up to me to take the steps to put the rest of the pieces of the puzzle together. And this book is one of the pieces that will be a part of the puzzle of my life as I live out my passion and purpose.

Sometimes following your passion means totally changing your life. Following a dream may mean that you have to step out of your present journey in order to follow the path of your passion. Perhaps you carefully design the path to change, or maybe the Universe throws a monkey wrench into "what is" so that you are free to create "what can be." Glenn is a good example of the latter.

He was fifty-two years old when the mortgage industry in which he had been working fell apart as our national economy headed downward. Glenn had always had a passion for food and cooking, and he had a dream of one day retiring and opening a small restaurant that served breakfast and lunch. But his dream began to seem unrealistic as he watched his income, his investments, and his financial stability slowly disappear. Yet Glenn and his wife knew that behind the catastrophe was an opportunity. And they took it! Glenn went back to school. He applied to the Le Cordon Bleu Cooking School and began his classes in November of 2009. In August of 2011, Glenn will have his degree and will have earned the professional title of Chef. Glenn is learning and living his passion! At the age of fifty-three he is a 4.0 student and already earning respect in his field. Glenn used his passion to change his life, and he's loving every minute of it.

The interesting thing about being willing to follow your passion is that when you take one step forward, opportunities that weren't there before start showing up. It's as though God or the Universe (whatever your faith may be) says, "Okay…you really want to do this, so we'll help." But you have to pay attention to be able to see the opportunities, and then you have to be willing to step forward and say "yes" to them. With your passion, determination, and persistence, you can move forward. You may not always move quickly or smoothly, but the journey will be filled with excitement because you are doing what you love.

Going back to school wasn't easy for Glenn. He had never been a student who had a desire to be at the top of his class. But that has changed! Glenn is now in the Honor Society and on the President's List, which opens up opportunities for volunteering at events where well-known Chefs like Mario Batalli, Paula Deen, and Bobby Flay are featured speakers and presenters. And Glenn works hard to make it all happen. But because he is following his passion, he does it with a smile.

And passion opens up the door for creativity. TerriAnn

discovered her love of writing when she was sixteen. Throughout the years TerriAnn kept diaries, written novels, and composed poetry...and it all went into file cabinets and boxes as TerriAnn pursued a career in business and used her writing skills in that arena. Last year, when TerriAnn turned sixty-one, her sister asked her how much longer she was going to wait to follow her passion. It was a good question, and it made TerriAnn realize that she had been making excuses and putting off doing what she wanted to do most in the world—to make a living by writing. That was a year ago, and TerriAnn is now making her living as a freelance writer and she will be publishing three of her own books this year. She will excitedly tell you that it is never too late, and even though your passion itself sometimes dictates when it will blossom, you can also be responsible for closing doors and preventing your passion from bursting into reality, as TerriAnn will freely admit that she had done.

"True...because I am older, I bring a fuller understanding and deeper dimension to everything I write," she says, "but I'll never know what I missed because I wasn't willing to take the risk and believe in myself and my own talents and abilities."

And it does take belief—in yourself, your abilities, or in God or a Higher Power who can and will guide you and help you when you get confused or off-track. But you ultimately get to decide, because if you are not willing to take that first step through the door, as TerriAnn readily agrees she wasn't willing to do, time will keep passing until you do.

When we're young and we discover our passion, lack of experience often prevents us from having the self-confidence to trust ourselves, our desires, and our dreams enough to move forward and create the kind of life we want. And as we get older, the years of experience that we have can hold us back because we know the price that life can sometimes exact from us. And as we age, we take on responsibilities and obligations to others, often putting our obligations and commitments to ourselves on a back burner or locking them away in a dark closet. If we've done this for enough years, we sometimes may not even know what we want or what we like, and have to spend some real time figuring that out.

What it comes down to is that you always have the choice not to let a lack of experience or too much experience with life determine whether you move forward with your dreams. The decision is yours. Start where you are. Live the process of finding and moving forward with your passion.

Sometimes in order to do that you have ascertain exactly what needs to be done for you to start on the journey of living your passion and loving your life. Once again, start with some questions:

o   Will I need education or training to be able to do what I really want to do (as in Glenn's case)?

o   Will it take a career change to follow my passion. If so, how can I build that change into my life?

o   Can I start slow by beginning with a hobby or part-time job, or by volunteering?

o   Do I already have skills that will help me step into the field I am passionate about? If so, can I now make the transition by using these skills?

And then take action:

o   **Research the different ways you can follow your passion.** There are probably many professions that involve what you are passionate about. For instance, Glenn could have gone in any of a number of different directions with his passion for food. He chose the one that held the greatest degree of excitement for him.

o   **Find a mentor.** Look for someone who is doing what you want to be doing. If you already know such a person, see if they will take you under their wing and give you direction, or even opportunities.

- o **Network** with people who are either in the field that you want to get into or have some connection with that field. Once you meet someone who can help, tell them about your passion and your dreams. Ask them if they have any suggestions for how you can get started. And be willing to listen to what they have to say.

- o **Let yourself be inspired** by someone or something. Julie Powell, author of the book Julie and Julia (which was also made into a film), was inspired by Julia Child. She decided to dedicate a year to making all of the 524 recipes in Julia Child's cookbook and then blog about it—while still keeping her full-time job. The project turned into a book and then a movie, simply because Julie Powell had a passion and she did something about it.

- o **Create a plan.** Even the greatest passion in the world needs some direction.

- o **Commit to something**... and get moving. Sometimes we can become paralyzed by inaction, and pretty soon our dreams and our passions start to wane.

- o **Gather a group of friends and brainstorm.** Let them in on what you want to do and see what ideas they may have that you haven't come up with yet.

o **Get training if you need it (or want it.** Don't let a lack of training or experience stop you. Find the training, get the experience (even if you have to go to school or work part-time while you keep your current job in order to keep a roof over your head).

If passion drives you,
let reason hold the reins.
~Benjamin Franklin

Don't expect everything to happen immediately. It's a process (I'll talk more about that in Chapter 9). Once you have discovered your passion, it is important that you take steps to move forward toward where you want to go. Bill Gates and Paul Allen didn't develop Microsoft into a billion-dollar company overnight. Jane Goodall, spent forty-five years studying chimpanzees.[11] Even Taylor Swift, who seems to have the world by the tail at the age of twenty, began writing songs at the age of five. So have a passion, have a dream, have a plan, and have patience.

If you are following your passion and you let the fires of possibility within you ignite, you will be willing and able to take the steps that need to be taken and follow the path wherever it leads you. Hyrum W. Smith, author of What Matters Most: The Power of Living Your Values,[12] states it well when he says, "You get that fire in your belly; you're willing to sacrifice for it; you're willing to take risks for it. And even when people tell you you've lost your mind, you don't back down."

I was able to see what I wanted to do,
I could see the opportunity,
even when others could not, and I
stayed committed to doing it and doing it well,
no matter what.

~Magic Johnson

CHAPTER 4

Stop Making Excuses

Professional skateboarder Tony Hawk,[6] is a perfect example of someone who followed his passion even though the journey wasn't always easy. Tony got his first skateboard when he was nine, and he turned pro at the age of fourteen. "When I was about seventeen, three years after I turned pro, my high school "careers" teacher scolded me in front of the entire class about jumping ahead in my workbook. He told me that I would never make it in the workplace if I didn't follow direction explicitly. He said I'd never make a living as a skateboarder, so it seemed to him that my future was bleak."

Tony is now a husband and father of three who has been a professional skateboarder for twenty-four years. He followed his passion no matter what others thought, and he continues to love and be proud of what he does. His passion is still strong because even though he now has many titles, including CEO and Executive Producer, "the (title) I am most proud of is 'Professional Skateboarder.' It's the one I write on surveys and customs forms, even though I often end up in a secondary security checkpoint."

Tony moved forward even though the going was not always easy. Many of us could learn a lot from his example because the majority of us will find myriad reasons not to follow our passion or do what we love—before we even try. We come up with a multitude of excuses and convince ourselves that they are actually valid reasons, when in reality, they're not. There is always a course of action that can be taken.

Take some time to pay attention to the thoughts that are holding you back from exploring or living your passion. Are you using some of the following excuses, or have you gotten really creative and invented ones that are even more detailed?

- o It's just not the right time.

- o I'll wait until my kids are out of school.

- o I'm too young to really know what my passion is.

- o I'm too old to follow my passion.

o   We just aren't in a financial spot for me to follow my passion.

o   I just don't think I have what it takes.

Somehow you've gotten the misconception that following your passion was going to be simple…that one day you'd wake up and a door would open with a big sign that says, "Today's the day you follow your passion," and the road would be well-marked and paved with gold. Nice fantasy, but it's a bit far from the reality. So you can continue to make excuses—many of which may certainly be valid—or you can gather up your courage, make a decision that this is what you are going to do, and move forward.

Rhynell has not let excuses get in his way. He is the author of The Go-Getter, and a poetic genius. There were famous poets from our past like Paul Lawrence Dunbar, James Weldon Johnson, Phyllis Wheatley, Langston Hughes. There are famous poets today who are sharing their poetic talents, such as Nikki Giovanni and Maya Angelou. And then came Rhynell, who has been writing poems and songs for well over twenty years. He wrote his first poem in the eighth grade because he was too shy to express his feelings verbally. That experience taught him to make poetry a vital part of how he communicates his thoughts, dreams, and ideas. He is a God-fearing man who expresses his views on life through his poetry. He is a poet at heart and a composer and songwriter in spirit.

Rhynell is a perfect example of a person of integrity and goodwill toward men. Rhynell is a people-person who loves helping others. He shows his gratitude for his success by helping at least two people each day. When others are hard at play, he is hard at work listening to inspirational CDs.

Rhynell is not only talented, but his mind holds a wealth of information. If you ask for his opinion on any given subject—especially starting a business—he will find the answer for you. He has inspired me to follow my dreams. Any time I needed encouragement, he would give me a motivational CD or book and say, "you'd better keep it moving."

His book of poems, The Go-Getter, is amazing and inspirational. Every spoken word is positive and from the heart, and he composes all of his own music. He has also made his poems available as an audio book. You can purchase a copy by visiting his Web site at rhynellwilliams.com

Although, Rhynell has become very successful, he gets his greatest fulfillment from living out his purpose for God and from his passion for helping others. Rhynell is the perfect example of someone who didn't let excuses cause him to fail.

Making excuses is just one of the forms of procrastination that many of us engage in on a daily basis. In the book, *The Now Habit: A Strategic Program for Overcoming Procrastination and Enjoying Guilt-Free Play*,[13] author Neil A. Fiore says that procrastination is really just a mechanism we use to resolve such underlying issues in our lives as:

o Low self-esteem
o Perfectionism
o Fear of failure (I'll talk more about defeating your fears in Chapter 6)
o Fear of criticism
o Fear of success
o Indecisiveness
o Imbalance between work and play
o Ineffective goal setting
o Fear of impossible expectations—in other words, feeling overwhelmed

So, if you are making excuses for your inability to live your passion or even discover what your passion is, the reason is that you're scared. But you can overcome your fear or low self-esteem. I love the saying, "How do you eat an elephant? One bite at a time!" And when life overwhelms me as it sometimes can, and I start procrastinating, I remember that phrase and take some steps to change my thought processes. Here are some that may work for you:

o **Pay attention to your self-talk.** Is it negative? Are you giving yourself a bunch of reasons why you can't move forward or won't succeed? If you are, change those messages in your mind to focus on all the reasons you can move forward and you will succeed.

o **When you find yourself making excuses or procrastinating, ask yourself why, and then listen closely to the answer.** If your answer is that you're scared, work through why you're scared and do what you have to do to assure yourself that it's okay, that you're okay, and that moving ahead will be good for you. If you're stuck for another reason, listen to the voice inside you to figure out what it is and what to do about it.

Once you realize that you are keeping yourself stuck by procrastinating and making excuses, do what you need to do to get moving forward. It is your passion and your life, so you get to be the one to decide how you're going to make this happen. The most important thing of all is that you have the desire to make it happen. Because if your passion is just an idea that resides in your head, it will probably stay there. But if it is an energy, an emotion, a drive that is deep within your heart and at the center of your very being, if it makes your heart race and your spirit soar whenever you think about it, if your passion is like a fetus in its mother's belly, it will be born!

So get excited about the birth of a new idea or a new way of life or a new journey that you are about to take part in, and stop making excuses. To borrow the Nike slogan, "Just Do It!"

Follow your passion
and success will follow you.
~Arthur Buddhold

CHAPTER 5

You have your Passion... Do you also have your Purpose?

I have often heard passion described as an energy or emotion that drives us, and purpose as the reason we are living right now on this earth. And I agree, because right now I have a passion for writing this book. But behind my passion is the purpose of helping others to discover, understand, and pursue their own passions and find their own purpose. In other words, purpose gives my passion a reason for being. Purpose is the built-in navigation system that keeps my passion on track and headed for the goal. My purpose is what my soul is on this earth to express or to accomplish. I believe that when our passion is connected with our purpose, life flows with meaning. That doesn't mean we won't have challenges or struggles or even setbacks, which are a part of living and learning, but it means that we are able to continue forward...purposefully.

Without purpose, passion would be like a football player without a goal post: he has just caught the football, he is excited about holding it snugly in his hands, but he has nowhere to go with it. His purpose isn't clear.

When your passion is combined with a purpose, there is a sense of direction—an innate navigation system—that keeps you on track and headed in a direction where your passion will have value and make a contribution, not only to your life, but to life as a whole. Having purpose gives you a sense of why you are on this earth and exactly what you are meant to do while you are here.

If you've discovered your passion, but there is no purpose behind it, your life could be like the colorful autumn leaves that blow from yard to yard when the wind comes up. Having no purpose, they are at the mercy of the wind, and they go in whatever direction it may blow them. And many people live their lives that way…going in whatever direction their current passion takes them or whatever direction the winds of life may blow them.

But people with passion and purpose have a course—a map, a reason, a direction—and it is solely and individually theirs because passion and purpose are personal! I'm talking about your life purpose…not an ego-driven purpose or a socially or financially driven purpose. For instance, my life's purpose is to make a difference in people's lives by helping them find their own passion and purpose. A financially-driven purpose might be to get rich; an ego-driven purpose might be to become famous. Purposes that come from our minds or our egos are external and can change on a dime, but a purpose that comes from our soul is steadfast and true.

Your purpose is about what you believe in—what your values are—the reason you believe that you are here in this lifetime. Purpose is about what you stand for, about your ideals. I think this quotation says it best:

Those who stand for nothing fall for anything.
~Alexander Hamilton

For me, when passion and purpose are united, it means that your heart is being directed by your soul. Your passion is being given a direction in which to go. And I believe that our purpose is waiting quietly within each of us for us simply to pay attention so that together with our passion, it can take us on the wonderful journey of life…as it is meant to be for each of us.

Passion and purpose go hand in hand.
When you discover your purpose,
you will normally find it's something
you're tremendously passionate about.
~Steve Pavlina

And I believe it also works in the other direction. When you find your heart-driven passion, your purpose is right below the surface, and as you begin pursuing your passion, your purpose will make itself known and clear.

My sister Jennifer discovered her passion at the age of four when she was dancing on my mom's dining room table. With a microphone in one hand and the other hand on her hips, she sang beautifully. And she continued to sing, completing her studies at the Duke Ellington School of Arts and at Bowie State University.

Then Jennifer discovered her purpose. She wanted young people to know that they could have a good time without using foul language or being inappropriately dressed...and Right Side Up Entertainment was formed. When Jennifer discovered that she had a gift for reaching young people, her purpose was quickly united with her passion.

www. empowerthepassionwithin.net

Her first show, Muslims Have Fun Too! was a variety show featuring the Believers of Mosque #4. And after Muslims Have Fun Too! II, a follow-up to the first show, Jennifer began to work with the Washington D.C. Public Schools, where she taught music, drama, dance, technical theater, and modeling. Her contracts later spread into Prince George's County, Maryland. During that time, company members performed at various churches, celebrations, and festivals.

In January of 2007, Right Side Up Entertainment held several events entitled Hurricane Healing, which helped victims of Hurricane Katrina. Hurricane Healing was a variety show featuring talent from Washington D.C. The show included singing, dancing, spoken word, rap, harp, and piano. The youngest member was two and the oldest was eighty. Among the nearly 400 audience members were twenty Katrina survivors. Hurricane Healing generated over $2,000 on behalf of the survivors, who said it felt good to know that they had not been forgotten.

Jennifer remembers that when she saw the news images of the devastation caused by Hurricane Katrina, she wanted to do something to help. That's when she was blessed with the vision to produce the show.

In 2008, she produced Hurricane Healing II, which was a huge success, and in the near future Jennifer hopes to purchase a building to house a children's musical theater company. Jennifer is living her passion and her purpose.

Do you know your heart's or life's purpose? Do you have an idea why you are here in this lifetime?

If you don't have a clue, don't be discouraged. There are several exercises you can do to bring your heart's purpose, which exists within you, to the surface. Begin by asking yourself a few questions:

- o What is my God-given talent or natural desire?

- o What legacy do I want to leave behind when I die? Do I want to be known for my abilities or talents—such as writing, painting, or speaking— or do I want to be remembered for my kindness, my thoughtfulness, and my thought-provoking ideas?

- o Have I done anything in my life so far that I feel was in alignment with my purpose?

Then, after you've asked yourself these questions, there are several exercises you can do to help your heart's purpose make its way to your consciousness:

- o **Start writing.** Take out a pen and paper and with those questions clearly planted in your mind, just start writing. Don't think about what you're writing and don't censor yourself; just let the thoughts and feelings flow from that place beyond the mind. And don't stop writing until you think you have nothing else to write…and then write a little bit more. Once you are done writing everything that has made its way to the paper from your mind, heart, and soul, read what you have written. Highlight the things that pop out and resonate for you. And once you've read everything you've written, look at what you've highlighted to see if there is a connection, a direction, a purpose in those highlighted phrases.

o   **Pray or meditate.** Ask for guidance from God (your Higher Power, the Ultimate Source). Surrender to that power that is larger than you, and be willing to learn your purpose and then to follow it. Once you have spent time in prayer or meditation, be aware of your thoughts, of things you see, or hear from other people, in songs, or in movies. Guidance can be sent in many different forms. Be open and you'll be surprised and delighted by what you receive.

o   **Use visualizations.** Take some quiet time and close your eyes. Picture yourself following your passion and watch where your passion leads you.

What does your life look like? Where are you? Taking time to visualize your future can give you some important clues to finding your purpose.

Finding and following your purpose is about becoming what you already are. You came into this life with a purpose. Once you allow that purpose to make itself known, you will be like the football player with the goal post in sight and the football in his hands. You will know exactly where you are headed, and although there may be obstacles in the way or hurdles that you have to jump over, your path will be well-defined.

Many people have the erroneous idea that discovering our passion and purpose means figuring out what we're really good at and then just doing it. Actually the experience can be totally opposite to that.

TerriAnn discovered her passion for writing at the age of sixteen, and several years later she realized that her purpose was to make a positive difference in people's lives through the written word. But TerriAnn wasn't yet a top-notch writer. Through the years she has learned that good writing is something that needs to be developed and crafted. The process hasn't been easy—rejections and criticism are part of the journey—and not everyone always understands what she is writing about or the way she is expressing it. But her passion and purpose stay with her every time she sits at her computer or puts pen to paper.

I think TerriAnn, like many other people who are following their passion and purpose, would tell you that the most important thing about having a passion and purpose is that they have given their life to something. There is more to their existence than just working, earning money, and being a consumer. It doesn't mean that those things aren't a part of their everyday existence, because they are. What it means is that working and consuming are not the reason they do what they do. Oprah once said that money was never the reason behind anything that she did—and we certainly all know that Oprah has plenty of money! She followed her passion and purpose and left the rest to the Universe!

As I put my thoughts down on paper and create this book, which is part of the journey of expressing my passion and following my purpose, I understand the importance of the journey. I've discovered that once I have my passion and my purpose, the journey is about overcoming obstacles (like fear), accepting challenges (like learning new skills), understanding that everything won't happen right at this very moment just because I want it to (timing) and that living my passion and purpose is truly about living out my potential in whatever form it may present itself.

If you are concentrating on results or if you have expectations, then you have not yet connected with the soul essence of your passion and purpose. I'm not saying that you shouldn't be aware of the need to provide for yourself and your family. I mean that you should hook on to your passion and purpose, make good decisions around the direction in which you are headed with them, and then put all your energy into creating what you love, what you believe in, and the reason you are living on this earth at this moment.

But also understand that what you do has value to others. One of the biggest mistakes that artists make is failing to understand that what they do has value. It's okay to charge for what you do. Oprah certainly understands the value of what she does! Advertisers don't get a spot on her show for free! Bill Gates doesn't give away Microsoft programs for free! Tiger Woods gets paid well to play golf, and Taylor Swift earns a nice living by writing songs and singing.

Your passion and purpose have a value to the world. Believe in yourself and believe in the gifts and talents that God gave you.

CHAPTER 6

Defeat Your Fear

D o you happen to know someone who has a deep passion for an idea, an action or even a skill, but the possibility of failure has stopped them before they can even get to the starting gate? They're not alone. Fear, whether it be of failure or of even trying, is probably the greatest barrier for most people who want to move forward in their lives and follow their passion.

In the book, Think & Grow Rich,[14] Napoleon Hill asserted that, "There are six basic fears, some combination of which every human suffers at one time or another. Most people are fortunate if they do not suffer from the entire six." These infamous six are poverty, criticism, ill health, loss of love of someone, old age, and death.

What are your fears? Are you stuck in one of the infamous six above, or have you created your own kind of fear that keeps you stuck doing what you feel you have to do instead of doing what you want to do? The first step toward defeating your fears is to take a good look at them. Confront the monster that is keeping you stuck, because until you do, you won't really know what you're up against.

- o **Name your fears.** There is a saying, "You have to name it to claim it," and it certainly applies when it comes to fear. So get real with yourself and look closely at what you are afraid of. Recognize it, analyze it, and put a name and shape to it.

- o **Make a list.** Write your fears down on paper so that they are no longer just in the recesses of your mind where they seem powerful and overwhelming. Putting them on paper reduces them to what they are—just thoughts.

- o **How real are they?** Let's say you have a fear that if you follow your passion, you and your family will starve to death and end up on the street. Okay, how real is that fear? Do you have financial resources that can help prevent that from happening? Will you do spot checks along the way and take a part-time job if you need to? Can you downsize your needs so that your monthly financial requirements are less? Are there steps and choices you can make to ensure that this doesn't happen? How real is this fear anyway?

o **Look at where your fears started.** Do your fears have a connection to your life now, or are they left over from things that you experienced in your childhood, in your adult past, or perhaps experiences that you have seen others go through? Or are they the result of a very active imagination?

o **Deal with the ones that have a connection to reality.** If any of your fears has a connection to the reality of your present life, then deal with it and create a safety net so that the fear cannot become a reality. For instance, maybe you are afraid of becoming sick and having everything you're planning for fall apart. If that's the case, take care of your health. If you have areas of concern, check them out and then take the steps you need to take to maintain good health. Eat a balanced diet, get some exercise, and keep yourself in a positive mental state. Do what you need to do to minimize the possibility of your fear becoming reality, and then step forward with faith.

o **Feel what you feel, but don't let negative feelings hold you back.** Remind yourself that feelings are not right or wrong, they just are, and feel your feelings. Okay, so you've got a little bit of fear going on right now. Acknowledge it, name it, claim it, deal with it, and then move forward.

Author Napoleon Hill also reminded us all that fears are "nothing more than states of mind," and that "Nature has endowed man with absolute control over but one thing, and that is thought."[14] In other words, you can change your mind and your life by changing your thoughts.

Fear melts when you take action
towards a goal you really want.
~Robert G. Allen

You have a choice: you can allow yourself to be caught up in fear and hold yourself back from creating the life that you desire, or you can change your negative thoughts into positive thoughts about what you can create, and figure out how you can do that. Here are some steps that can help you change your thoughts, keep your fears in check, and in the process change your life.

○ **Get focused.** Figure out what you really want to do. Make your plan. Think about whether you can follow your passion now or whether it is something that you can work toward. Focus on that. Take steps toward creating the life that you desire.

o **Make a decision to do it.** If you are wishy-washy about your intent and what you want to do, your actions will be just as wishy-washy, so decide to do it…and then do it!

o **Make your own luck.** Don't sit back and wait for something to happen. Instead, understand that when you stay focused and move forward, opportunities will open up that will allow you to move closer to your goal. But you've got to take the first step. Show God and the Universe that you are really serious and passionate about this. It's your move!

o **Take small steps.** You don't have to accomplish in one day, week, month, or year everything that needs to be done in order to live your passion. Take small steps toward your ultimate goal and celebrate each step you take (I'll talk more about this process in Chapter 9).

o **Be willing to take risks when necessary.** You won't get from here to there if you are not willing to take the risk of that first step.

o **Stay positive.** You have to believe in yourself and what you are doing. Other people can't do that for you. If you wait for approval from others, you may be waiting a long time, because everyone else is caught up in their own lives, passions, fears, and challenges.

o **Mistakes will happen.** And when they do, they are not a "sign" that you shouldn't be pursuing your dreams; they are simply a part of life, and sometimes they have very important lessons to teach that will help you throughout the rest of your life. So don't let mistakes overwhelm or discourage you. Look closely and see what you can learn from them.

o **Be persistent.** If you really want it bad enough, you will stay focused and continue moving forward even if setbacks occasionally occur.

o **Keep your passion at the forefront.** Never forget your passion and what you love to do. Keep that always at the forefront of your mind when fears or doubts creep in.

o **Stay connected with the present moment.** Don't get caught up in the past r in the future. Stay in the present and aware of what the reality is at this moment. Your power to make decisions is in this moment. You can't change what happened in the past, but you can learn from it. And you don't have any control of what could happen in the future, but you can take steps at this moment to positively influence what may happen. Your power of choice is in this moment, right now!

o **Have Faith.** In yourself and in God, your Higher Power.

Having faith is the most important step of all. Napoleon Hill's book, Think & Grow Rich,[14] was written between 1908 and 1937 and resulted from his observations about five hundred of the most successful people in the world. The interesting thing is that the tools and strategies that were used by successful people in the early twentieth century are still being used by prosperous and famous people today, and a recurring theme throughout Hill's book is the importance of connecting with God (also referred to as a Higher Power or Creative Force). Although belief systems are individual and private choices, the importance of a connection with the Ultimate Source of all things is as important today as it was for people in the 1900s who were following their dreams and passions.

As you move forward to conquer your fear and follow your passion, staying connected with your faith helps to keep you focused (I talk more about the importance of faith in Chapter 8). Faith, like anything else that is important to us, must be given regular time and attention. These habits or routines must be built into your daily life in order to help you stay connected. If you defeat your fear, you can live your passion and the life that you dream about.

- **Pray or meditate.** Spend some time in quiet contemplation with your thoughts, ideas, and hopes and share them with God.

- **Keep a journal.** Put your thoughts and desires on paper. Often when we write, our subconscious mind can overcome the fears of our conscious mind.

- **Have an attitude of gratitude.** In his book, Gratitude: A Way of Life,[15]John Randolph Price makes the observation that, "When we live with grateful hearts, fear cannot enter, guilt is dissolved, and there is only peace, love, forgiveness, and understanding. To me, that's what life is all about."

- **Surround yourself with people who have positive attitudes and faith** in life, in themselves, in God. Keeping people with positive attitudes in your life will make maintaining your own faith and optimism much easier.

- **Ask for help and support** from God and from the positive people in your life.

And then move forward! Sometimes we get into the habit of being afraid of life, or afraid of anything new or different, so we stay exactly where we are instead of moving forward toward whatever the future holds.

Shame on us! We were created to be magnificent, to live life to its fullest and to make a difference, even if it is just in our small world. Author Marianne Williams challenges us all by making some strong statements and asking some very poignant questions:

Our Deepest Fear
By Marianne Williamson

Our deepest fear is not that we are inadequate.
Our deepest fear is that we are powerful beyond measure.
It is our light, not our darkness, that most frightens us.

We ask ourselves, who am I to be brilliant, gorgeous,
talented and fabulous?
Actually, who are you not to be?

You are a child of God.

Your playing small does not serve the world.
There is nothing enlightened about shrinking
so that other people won't feel insecure about you.
We are all meant to shine, as children do.
We were born to manifest the glory of God that is within us.
It's not just in some of us, it's in everyone.

And as we let our own light shine,
we unconsciously give other people permission to do the

same.
As we are liberated from our own fear,
our presence automatically liberates others.

Sometimes we need people in our lives to help us overcome our fears and to help us understand that "playing small" does not serve any purpose. My biggest supporter and motivator has been my husband. Whenever I have an idea, he tells me to go for it. If there is any doubt in my mind, he encourages me to keep going and figure out how I can get there. He has never once told me that my dream was impossible. He is always supportive and positive. His motto is, "there is no try, it is only do or do not." He is a God-fearing man who leads by example and is the perfect role model for our sons.

So…what about you? Are you ready to be done "playing small"? Are you ready to step forward and let your light shine? If you need someone to be there for you and encourage you, then find them. Whether it's a spouse, a parent, a friend, or someone famous whom you can watch from afar, there are people who are willing and able to help you defeat your fear and live your passion.

CHAPTER 7

Never Stop Learning

When you are ready to follow your passion and purpose, you may know everything you need to know to move forward, but most likely you won't. Our passions may be for things we're interested in, but we always have more to learn about them. Sometimes that learning will take the form of formal education and sometimes it won't.

Knowledge is power, and knowledge comes from learning, so sometimes a formal education is the best choice. For instance, when Glenn decided that he wanted to follow his passion for food and his purpose of someday having his own restaurant, he knew that he wanted formal training to enable him to become the best Chef he could be and to learn how to operate a successful restaurant. So Glenn is going to school, where he will learn all of that and more.

But depending on how you learn and what you need to learn, other forms of learning may be even more effective for you. Picasso turned down the chance for a formal art education in Madrid, preferring to live and learn in the strongly art-influenced atmosphere of Paris. And many well-known people—including Director Quentin Tarantino, actors Johnny Depp, Nicholas Cage, Jim Carrey, and John Travolta, and Wendy's founder Dave Thomas—have dropped out of school.[16] All these people went on to follow their passions and became very wealthy and well known. Just because they didn't pursue learning in a formal setting doesn't mean they didn't continue to learn and become skilled at their craft and their passion.

Seventeen-year-old Hillary is passionate about helping children, and has decided to become a pediatrician specializing in Oncology. Hillary's passion and purpose will require a lot of formal education and experience.

Thirteen-year-old Tessa loves sports of all kinds. She isn't sure what she wants to do with her passion, and she doesn't know her purpose yet, but she knows that although she will pursue an education, excelling in sports will require a lot of practice.

Learning should be a life-long pursuit, whether iin a formal setting or through reading, listening, experiencing, and traveling. The best way for you to learn depends on what your passion and purpose are, and how you learn best. There are many ways to learn, which we'll discuss a bit later in this chapter. First of all, it's important for you to understand how you learn best so that you can make the right choices when it comes to preparing to follow your passion and live your purpose.

Styles of Learning

There are three styles of learning:[17]

1. By Seeing (Visual)

2. By Listening (Auditory)

3. By Touching or Experiencing (Kinesthetic & Tactile)

If you know that you learn best by experiencing something, then sitting all day in a class listening to a lecture probably isn't going to teach you what you need to learn, and it certainly won't be much fun for you. If you learn best by listening, you won't benefit from someone handing you an instruction manual and expecting you to memorize it and do what it says.

If you're not sure which learning style is best suited for you, ask yourself a few questions:[18]

1. When you read, do you…

   a. Like scenes that are described in detail or do you often pause to imagine the actions in your mind?
   b. Enjoy a lot of dialog and conversation in the story or can you hear the characters talking?
   c. Prefer stories with a lot of action or do you not enjoy reading very much at all?

2. When you are required to learn something new at work, how do learn most easily?

   a. From demonstrations, diagrams, slides or posters?
   b. From verbal instructions or discussion with someone else?
   c. By just jumping right in and trying the new process or procedure?

3. When you need to contact someone regarding business, do you…

   a. Prefer to set up face-to-face meetings?
   b. Typically prefer to use the telephone?
   c. Set up an activity that will allow you to talk

with them while being engaged in doing something together?

If you answered "a" for all the questions above, you have a visual style of Learning. If your answers were all "b," you are an auditory learner, and if they were all "c," you learn best by touching and experiencing; in other words, you are a kinesthetic and tactile learner.

If your answers to the above questions didn't stay in the A, B, or C categories, and you just aren't sure what learning style best suits you, this Web site offers a free survey to help you figure that out:

http://people.usd.edu/~bwjames/tut/learning–style/stylest.html

The type of education you pursue will not only have a lot to do with what you want to learn and how you learn best, it will also depend on where you are in your life and the kind of education you have had up to this point.

It is crucial, however, that you don't let age or financial status deter you from getting the education or training you need to follow your passion. Often people will use their age or their financial condition as an excuse for not doing what they want to do. Excuses are usually based in fear, so screw up your courage, decide on the type of education you need, and then figure out how you can pay for it.

Types of Education

There are many different ways to acquire training to do what you want to do.

- Higher education at a college or university
- College courses in high school
- Community technical or vocational college
- Vocational/skill training schools
- Online degrees or certificates
- On-the-job training
- Apprenticeships
- Continuing education

The important first step is deciding what type of education or training you need, looking at all the options available to help you get that education, and finally choosing the one that is going to work best for you.

Ways To Pay For Education

Whether you are still in high school, in the middle of your life, or preparing to retire, there are a variety of ways to fund any education you may need in order to pursue your passion and purpose:

o **Grants and scholarships:** These are funds that you don't have to pay back. Often they are given one semester at a time. Every educational institution has staff whose job it is to help students determine whether they are eligible for these funds.

o **Student loans:** This is money you borrow that will need to be repaid—typically after you finish your education and are gainfully employed.

o **Parent loans:** If you are just graduating from high school, the Federal Family Education Loan allows parents to borrow funds to make up the difference between any financial aid you may be eligible for and the cost of the school you have chosen.

o **Work study:** Many schools have programs that allow students to work either at the school or with businesses that offer jobs to students enrolled at the school. Through these programs, students can earn money for tuition and other expenses they incur while pursuing their education.

o **Federal funding:** A great deal of educational funding comes from the United States government, and eligibility is ascertained by filling out the FAFSA Form (Free Application for Federal Student Aid), which can be found at *www.fafsa.ed.gov* This site also has a link to the U.S. Department of Education, where additional resources for educational funding can be found. The information on the FAFSA is based on the applicant's most recent income tax return.

After the FAFSA is filled out, the government will calculate your expected contribution and send a report to you and to the schools of your choice. The school you select can then figure out what other funding may be needed and available for you.

○ **Workforce incentive programs:** Many states have these programs for people who are pursuing education in areas in which the state has a shortage of qualified candidates. Do a search on the Internet to discover whether your state offers any of these incentives. Areas of study such as foreign language, nursing, or special education are often covered in these programs.

○ **Funds for veterans or orphans of veterans:** If you have served in the U.S. military or if you are a student between the ages of sixteen and twenty-five whose parent died in the course of military service, special funding may be available. Check with your local VA office.

o **Business scholarships offered by private groups:** There are a variety of national professional associations that offer business school scholarships. Check out each individual organization for more information:

- American Marketing Association
- Business and Professional Women's Foundation
- National Business Association
- National Society of Accountants
- National Association for the Self Employed
- National Black MBA Association

o **Other funding and scholarship help:** Many organizations and foundations offer scholarships to people of all ages. These are just a few:

- **Jeannette Rankin Foundation, Inc.** Technical/ vocational or undergraduate programs for women thirty-five years or older *http://rankinfoudnation.org*

- **Fannie and John Hertz Foundation Graduate Fellowships:** For people working toward a Ph.D. in a scientific field. *www. hertzfndn.org/fields.html*

- **Women in Aviation International**

Scholarships: For women pursuing an education in aviation or engineering. _www. wai.org/education/scholarships.cfm_

- **Women's Sport Foundation** Scholarship and funding options for women who are pursuing careers in sports. _www. womenssportsfoundation.org/_

- **Bill and Melinda Gates Foundation** _www. gatesfoundation.org/topics/Pages/scholarships. aspx_

- **Marine Corps Scholarship Foundation:** Available to children or grandchildren of current or former U.S. Marines. _www. marine-scholars.org_

These are just a few of the many scholarships available through a wide variety of sources. Talk with a counselor at the school you choose or search the Internet.

Additional Resources

The following Web sites provide information and assistance for exploring different careers, as well as education and training:

Career Information - *www.careeronestop.com*

Education, Jobs and Volunteerism for Seniors - *www. usa.gov/Topics/Seniors/Education.shtml*

Financial Aid Information for Women – *www.finaid.org*

Help with finding scholarships - *www.fastweb.com*

Areas of Education, Training or Learning

There are many areas of learning, and many educational opportunities in each area.

This is a general listing of fields and some of the careers that are possible in each of them:

- o **Arts & Creative**

  - Actors
  - Announcers
  - Artists
  - Camera operators and editors
  - Choreographers
  - Dancers
  - Fashion designers
  - Graphic designers
  - Interior designers
  - Musicians

- Photographers
- Producers
- Singers
- Religion
- Writers and editors

o **Business**

- Accounting
- Management
- Business Administration
- Business Communications
- Business Information Systems
- Business Leadership
- Business Specializations
- Conflict Management
- Customer Service
- e-Business and e-Commerce
- Economics
- Finance
- Hotel and Hospitality Management
- Human Resources
- International Business
- Management
- Marketing
- Operations Management
- Organizational Management
- Project Management
- Real Estate

- Risk Management
- Small Business Management
- Sports Management

o **Computer & I.T.**

- Computer Science and Engineering
- Computer Security
- Databases
- Game Design
- Graphics and Multimedia
- Information Systems
- Information Technology
- Networks
- Programming
- Software Engineering
- Technology Management
- Telecommunications
- Web Design
- Web Development

o **Education & Teaching**

- Adult and Higher Education
- Curriculum and Instruction
- Distance Education
- Early Childhood Education
- Educational Administration
- Educational Counseling

- Educational Leadership
- Educational Technology
- English as a Second Language
- General Education
- K–12 Education
- Library and Resource Management
- Special Education

o **Health & Medicine**

- Alternative Medicine
- Anesthetists
- Audiologists
- Biomedical Engineers
- Cardiovascular Technologists and Technicians
- Chiropractors
- Counseling
- Dentists
- Dental Hygienists
- Dental Laboratory Technicians
- Diagnostic Medical Sonographers
- Dieticians
- Emergency Medical Technicians
- Fitness
- Health Administration
- Health Science
- Health Services
- Home Healthcare
- Human Services

- Language Pathologists
- Medical Assistants
- Medical Billing
- Medical Information
- Medical Office
- Medical Scientists
- Medical Transcription
- Midwives
- Nuclear Medicine Technologists
- Nursing
- Nutritionists
- Occupational Therapy
- Ophthalmic Laboratory Technicians
- Opticians
- Optometrists
- Paramedics
- Pharmacists
- Physical Therapy
- Physicians
- Physician Assistants
- Psychology
- Public Health
- Radiology
- Recreational Therapists
- Respiratory Therapists
- Social Workers
- Surgeons
- Surgical Technologists
- Veterinary Medicine

○ **Science & Engineering**

- Aerospace Engineers
- Agricultural Engineers
- Agricultural Scientists
- Atmospheric Scientists
- Aviation
- Biological Scientists
- Broadcast Engineering Technicians
- Chemical Engineers
- Chemists and Materials Scientists
- Civil Engineers
- Engineering Management
- Environmental Engineers
- Environmental Scientists
- Food Scientists
- Forensic Sciences
- Geological Engineers
- Geoscientists
- Industrial Engineers
- Materials Engineers
- Mathematicians
- Mechanical Engineers
- Mining Engineers
- Mining Safety Engineers
- Nuclear Engineers
- Petroleum Engineers
- Physicists
- Quality Control

o **Social Sciences**

- Criminal Justice
- History
- Homeland Security
- Law
- Legal Studies
- Paralegal
- Political Science
- Public Administration
- Public Safety
- Sociology

o **Trades & Careers**

- Administrative Assistant
- Agricultural Managers
- Animal Care
- Appliance Repair
- Automotive and Mechanics
- Bridal Consulting
- Carpentry and Construction
- Child Day Care
- Construction and Building Inspectors
- Construction Managers
- Cosmetology
- Culinary
- Drafting
- Electronics

- Forestry and Wildlife
- HVAC
- Landscaping
- Plumbing and Electrical
- Private Investigator
- Security
- Travel and Tourism
- Wedding Planning

This is just a general listing of careers and career categories to get you started on thinking in detail about what direction you need to take and what training or education you will need.

If your passion or field of interest isn't covered, check with a career counselor or search the Internet to find more information on educational opportunities.

Life As Your Teacher

Whatever other education you may have, it is very important to understand that life is the best teacher we will ever have. Some of our best lessons are learned from the experiences we have and the people we meet along the way. Embrace those experiences and lessons as you move forward with living your passion and purpose.

Develop a passion for learning.
If you do, you will never cease to grow.
~Anthony J. D'Angelo

CHAPTER 8

The Importance of Faith

A strong part of having faith is believing that we have a reason for being in this lifetime, exactly when and where we are. The challenge is to continue to believe as we try to identify and understand that purpose. Whether you are religious or spiritual or a combination of both, following your life purpose connects with your belief system. The need to have a purpose comes from our soul—that part of us that is at the center of who we are.

I am led by faith. I believe that I have a purpose in this world and that God puts people and experiences in my path to help me find and live that purpose. And when the timing is right—when I have finally surrendered and said "yes" to God's consistent knocking at the door of my heart—what I need will be there when I need it.

I am consistently reminded that God is always at work and that he often works in mysterious ways. For instance, I always knew that I wanted to help people, but I didn't know in what capacity. Then one day I was talking to my friend Cynthia, who is the Director of my son's daycare, about how I did not like the fact that many kids were but not getting the financial assistance they needed to go to college. At that time I had several girlfriends whose children were attending college and struggling with this issue, so I decided to do some research on finding grants for them. I thought, How hard could it be? In the course of my research I discovered that there are plenty of grants available, but locating the information is very time-consuming.

Several months later, Cynthia asked me if I would speak to her "girls" about going to college. She had started a group called The Royal Diamonds, comprising a number of girls between the ages of fourteen and nineteen who have had some challenges, but were walking in a life with Christ and who were determined to be a true light in this world.

When Cynthia asked me to speak to her group, I immediately said yes, but I was unsure why she had asked me to speak on this subject and whether I was qualified to do it. Little did I know that this would lead me to a journey of helping children.

Once I had accepted Cynthia's invitation, I had to prepare a presentation. I quickly turned to my sister, who is a drama teacher, for help. The presentation came together nicely. It was well-received by the The Royal Diamonds, and it inspired me to write this book and to live out my passion for helping young people.

Faith isn't the ability to believe long and far into the misty future.
It's simply taking God at his word and taking the next step.
                                        Joni Erickson Tada

Sometimes faith easily combines with living our passion. We feel that the timing is right and we know what we love and what we are meant to do. At other times, we know what we are passionate about and we believe that we know our purpose, but it's hard to take the steps to bring those two things into the reality of our everyday life. It's hard to believe that something we want so badly will really come to pass. If that's the case for you, there are steps that you can take to strengthen your faith and connect it with your passion and your purpose. Whether your faith is religious or spiritual at its core, connecting with God (Your Higher Power, The Ultimate Source) can help you live your passion and your purpose every day. These are steps that you can take to use the power of your faith to help you.

- Become open to the possibility that God created you specifically for this purpose and that's why you feel the passion you feel.

- Let God be your source of power. When you are feeling doubtful, scared, or defeated, spend time in prayer or meditation to strengthen your faith.

- Spend some time really getting to know who you are, paying attention to your strengths and talents, accepting that God gave you these gifts to help you live your passion and purpose.

- Strengthen your talents as your way of showing God that you are grateful for these gifts and for being who you are.

- Have an "attitude of gratitude." Be thankful for every day—even those that are challenging. As you spend time in gratitude, you'll find that the challenges become less overwhelming as you move through them in the process of living your passion.

- When your path gets foggy, ask for God's guidance in clearly defining what you are intended to do and the direction you are intended to take.

- Understand that you are a magnificent creation

with a passion and purpose that is uniquely yours. And by living this passion, you will bring joy and fulfillment not only to your own life, but to the lives of those you will touch and interact with.

o Show compassion and love to others. Remember, as we give, we receive.

Pastor and author, Howard Clinebell[19] believed that there are seven spiritual hungers that all people have in common.

1. Everyone needs to experience, on an ongoing basis, the healing and empowerment of love from themselves, from others, and from an ultimate source (i.e., God).

2. We all need renewing times of transcendence that expand us beyond our immediate sensory spheres.

3. Everybody needs beliefs that give them a sense of meaning and hope.

4. We all need to have values, priorities, and life commitments that guide us in personally and socially responsible living. Those values are usually love, justice, and integrity.

5. Every human being needs to discover and develop their inner wisdom, creativity, and love of their unique spiritual self.

6. We all need to cultivate a deep awareness of our oneness with other people and with the natural world, the wonderful web of all living things.

7. Everybody needs spiritual resources to heal painful wounds and to deepen our experiences of trust, self-esteem, hope, and joy.

Whatever it means to you and however you connect with God (your Higher Power or Ultimate Source), faith is an important part of living your passion and purpose. Faith helps you believe that you do have a purpose in this lifetime and that the things you love to do and are passionate about are God-given talents.

Faith is not only an important part of following your passion and purpose, it is often your strongest tool for helping you live life to your fullest potential.

CHAPTER 9

It's the Process that Counts

Most of us want to hurry through life's experiences to get to whatever we consider to be the end product or "bottom line." But life is about the process, and when you are first discovering and living your passion and your purpose, the process is what really counts.

In the book, Your Best Life Now,[20] Joel Osteen presents seven steps for improving your life right now, wherever you are:

1. Enlarge your vision
2. Develop a healthy self image
3. Discover the power of your thoughts and words
4. Let go of the past
5. Find strength in adversity
6. Live to give
7. Choose to be happy

I totally agree with every one of these steps. My perception of what these steps mean is as follows:

1. **Enlarge your vision.** Make your dream, your vision as large as you can possibly imagine. Don't think small because you believe you have to. I just watched a video of the show Britain's Got Talent, on which an eighty-year-old great-great-grandmother got on the stage and sang her heart out. Her voice was amazing! She didn't think small because she was concerned that she was too old. She didn't worry about whether it was "past her time." The opportunity presented itself, she went for it, and she was a huge hit! What is the biggest dream you can dream?

2. **Develop a healthy self image.** Your self image is at the core of everything you do. If you don't really believe in yourself or your capabilities, you're going to have a hard time believing in your passion and purpose and building your life around them. So if your self image needs some work, do what you have to do to think and feel better about yourself.

3. **Discover the power of your thoughts and words.** Listen to your thoughts. Whether you are aware of them or not, they dictate your actions and your behaviors. Are your thoughts negative, telling you

that you won't be able to do what you want to do? Or are your thoughts positive, encouraging and full of hope?

4. **Let go of the past.** Are you hanging on to past experiences that you consider unsuccessful? If so, these experiences could be holding you back from taking the steps you need to take in order to live your passion.

5. **Find strength in adversity.** Don't be afraid of challenges! They make us strong. If you meet obstacles, move through them. Think of them as building blocks or stones in a pathway that you handle one at a time as you head toward your goal.

6. **Live to give.** Show kindness to others along the way. As you help others, you build empathy and compassion, which are good life-long companions for living your passion and purpose.

7. **Choose to be happy.** Happiness really is a choice. Often people make excuses for not being happy, just like they make excuses for not following their passions. But remember, the way you approach and live life is a choice. I love the saying, "Life is ten percent about what happens to us and ninety percent about how we handle it." So make the

choice to be happy each moment as you move forward and live your passion.

Yet in order to be able to do the seven things that Osteen recommends, it's important to get back to the basics of life. If your body, mind, and spirit are not being cared for and in very top form, it will be hard to have the energy or enthusiasm to move forward and live your life at your full potential.

Sometimes when we have connected with our passion and are following our purpose, we become so focused on those two aspects of our lives that we neglect the rest of us. But remember, we are many-faceted beings with bodies, minds, and spirits—and our lives have many facets to them as well. Passion and purpose are definitely at the core of who we are, but there are many aspects that surround and support those core beliefs.

So take some time and look at your daily habits to see if you are taking care of yourself. If you are not, think about what you need to do on a daily basis to be the best that you can be. This will allow you to follow your passion and live out your purpose.

o **The food you eat.** What are your eating habits? Do you grab something on the go when you feel hungry, without paying attention to what you are eating and when? If so, it's time to slow down and pay attention to whether you are providing your body with the nutrition it needs. Do you eat plenty of fruits and vegetables? How much water do you drink each day? Remember, the food you put in your body is like the fuel you put in your vehicle: if you are putting in low-grade fuel with contaminants in it, your vehicle isn't going to run well. The same goes for your body. Feed it well with healthy, nutritious food and it will respond by giving you the energy and concentration you need when you need it.

o **Your level of activity.** Your body needs movement, and when you give it the right level of activity, even your mind and spirit are positively affected. The ideal level of activity is different for each one of us. Perhaps you respond best to gentle movement like yoga or Tai Chi. Or you may be someone who benefits from going to a gym and working out on the equipment. Then again, walking could be the best form of movement and activity for you. Since following your passion and purpose is all about getting to know yourself, spend some time discovering what type and level of movement works best for you and then make time in each day to engage in it.

o **Rest is important.** How many times have you complained that, "There aren't enough hours in the day," and then taken the extra hours you needed out of the time that you should be resting? Many of us do this much too often, and the consequences catch up with us. Sleep and rest are important. Some of us do best on seven hours of sleep, but some of us need eight, nine or ten hours. Pay attention to your body and how much rest it needs, and then get it. And your needs for rest and sleep may change. If you are paying attention to your body, you'll know when to make adjustments.

o **What about your emotional health?** I recently heard the term "emotional chaos," meaning, "any time you are not peaceful or joyful." Thinking of our emotions from that perspective, most of us experience some "emotional chaos" on a daily basis. When this happens to you, take a moment and ask yourself why. Are you disconnected from your heart and spirit? Are you trying to do or be something that is not a part of who you are? Have you procrastinated and put yourself into a state of emotional chaos by falling behind on deadlines or important tasks? Are you beating up on yourself because "perfectionism" is rearing its ugly head? Whenever you do not feel a sense of peace and joy, take a moment to ask yourself what emotions you are feeling, and why. Then answer your question and do what you need to do to get yourself back to feeling centered, peaceful, and joyful.

o **Honor your mind/body/spirit connection.** Take a few moments each day to connect with God and to thank him for your gifts and talents and for the people, and even the challenges, that come into your life each day. Be grateful for your alert, creative mind and your healthy, strong body. Take responsibility for every part of you, embrace all of who you are, and love your total self.

Even though challenges will arise from time to time, following your passion will give you a purpose for your life and a sense that your actions and your life are having an impact on others. And as you live each day to the fullest, you will enjoy following your passion and purpose, and you will enjoy every moment of every day of your life!

Our passions are the winds that propel our vessel.
Our reason is the pilot that steers her.
Without winds the vessel would not move
and without a pilot she would be lost.
~Proverb

CHAPTER 10
Live Out Your Potential

You are a precious creation, living on this earth at this particular time in order to fulfill a special purpose. You've been given the gifts and talents that you need to fulfill that purpose, and you are endowed with passion for those talents. Now it's time to move forward! You have your passion, you understand your purpose, and you are done making excuses…right?

Good! That means that you are in alignment and able to fully live your potential, no matter how young or old you are or where you are in your life. Continue to live to your full potential by developing these healthy habits:

- o **Live in the moment.** Life is about each moment as it is happening. Don't get so caught up in yesterday or tomorrow that you miss the precious moment that you are living right now. Your choices and your power are in the now, so live each day and each moment consciously.

○ **Be humble.** As you move forward with your passion and purpose and doors in life start to open for you, stay in your spirit instead of letting your ego take over and make it all about you. Let your decisions be guided by your faith and humility instead of by your ego.

○ **Believe in yourself.** If you don't believe in yourself, it will be difficult for others to believe in you. Even when challenges arise, believe that you can rise above any obstacle you meet along the way to living out your potential. Remember the story of the little choo-choo train and its mantra, "I think I can...I think I can...I think I can...I must!" There's another saying that helps me when I begin to doubt myself... "Whether we think we can or think we can't, we're right!"

There is no passion to be found playing small—in settling for a life that is less than the one you are capable of living.
~Nelson Mandela

○ **Stay on target.** You have a passion and purpose that are unique to you. Don't let the opinions and attitudes of others take you off your path or your targeted goals. Be true to yourself. Remember what you want in your life and the reason you want it.

o **Follow your natural instinct for wanting to make a difference** in your own life and in the lives of those with whom you interact as you move forward with your passion and purpose.

o **Remember that you can learn from the purpose of another, but stay true to your own passion and purpose.** Every one of us has a combination of passion and purpose that is unique to us. Along your path you will meet others who will inspire you and even help you, but remember that their passion and purpose is theirs, and your passion and purpose is the path that you are intended to follow. So learn from others, but don't imitate them.

o **Always be who you are when nobody else is looking.** Are there two of you? The person you try to be when other people are around and the person you are when you are all by yourself? Find the real you and then stick with that person no matter where you are or who you are with. You are exactly enough just as you are!

o **The power is always within you.** Whether you

need to make new choices, learn new skills, find a new mentor, reach out to others, or whatever else you may need to do in order to live out your potential, you always have the power within you to make it happen.

Above all, be true to yourself, and if you cannot put your heart in it, take yourself out of it.
~Author Unknown

o **Keep your attitude of gratitude.** When you are grateful for exactly where you are in life, you have the enthusiasm to move forward to where you want to be.

o **Surround yourself with positive, supportive people.** The people in our lives are reflections of what we truly believe about life. So surround yourself with loving, positive, supportive, people to help you stay on track.

o **Take responsibility for your life.** Your choices and your actions create your life, so if you don't like who you are, where you are, or what is happening in your life, change it! The people who hold themselves accountable for their lives are the ones who live to their absolute fullest potential. So take responsibility!

o **Be willing to help others to discover their passion and purpose.** As you follow your passion and purpose, be willing to share your experiences with others along the way. As we help others achieve their goals and dreams, we achieve our own.

o **Manage your stress.** Stress happens, and it can have a negative effect on our bodies if we don't take the time to address the "fight or flight" response that stress provokes in our bodies. So take time to pray, play, laugh, be silly, and unwind. Following your passion and purpose should be a fun experience. A focused life doesn't have to be a totally serious life.

o **Stay balanced in your connection of body, mind, and spirit.** In Chapter 9 I talked about taking care of yourself, which is essential to being able to live out your full potential. Without a healthy body, mind and spirit you will not be able to fully embrace and experience your passion and purpose.

The most important phrase to remember if you want to live out your potential is, "To your own self be true." Remember, your potential is yours alone…it is different from anyone else's. As you live your life, you will meet people who believe that they know exactly what your passion and purpose should be, or how you can best reach your full potential. Listening never hurts, because they may have some wonderful insights for you, but listening to what others say and doing exactly what they recommend are two entirely different things.

Living your full potential means just that: living every moment in every day. Living requires action and doing. You can't just think your passion and purpose into being; you must take steps to make it happen and bring it all together. Sometimes you may takes steps or actions that don't bring you the results that you wanted; but that's okay, because in every step or action there is a lesson or an accomplishment that helps you become wiser, kinder, more compassionate, more skilled, or in some way a little bit better than you were before you took that step.

RESOURCES

1. Tiger Woods' Biography.
   www.starpulse.com/Athletes/Woods,_Tiger/Biography/

2. From Young Cook to KFC's Famous Colonel.
   www.kfc.com/about/colonel.asp

3. Pablo Picasso Biography.
   www.answers.com/topic/pablo-picasso

4. Pablo Picasso Biography/Autobiography/Memoir
   Resources. *www.biographyshelf.com/pablo_picasso_biography.html*

5. Taylor Swift Biography.
   www.people.com/people/taylor_swift/biography

6. Tony Hawk. Article, Do What You Love.
   www.npr.org/templates/story/story.php?storyId=5568583

7. Bill Gates. Article, Unleashing the Power of Creativity. *www.org.npr.org/templates/story/story.php?storyId=4853839&ps=rs*

8. Article, Andrea Bocelli, opera singer. *ww.classicalx.com/article2828.html*

9. Mary Wesley. *http://en.wikipedia.org/wiki/Mary_Wesley*

10. Julia Child Biography. *www.biography.com/articles/Julia-Child-9246767*

11. Jane Goodall. *http://en.wikipedia.org/wiki/Jane_Goodall*

12. Smith, Hyrum W. What Matters Most: The Power of Living Your Values. (New York: Fireside. 2000)

13. Fiore, Neil A. The Now Habit: A Strategic Program for Overcoming Procrastination and Enjoying Guilt-Free Play. (New York: Jeremy P. Tarcher/Putnam, 1989)

14. Hill, Napoleon. Think & Grow Rich. (New York. Barnes & Noble, Inc. 2008. Originally published 1937.)

15. Hay, Louise L. and Friends. Gratitude A Way of Life. (California: Hay House, Inc. 1996)

16. Article, 10 Famous Millionaire High School Dropouts!
http://socyberty.com/people/10-famous-millionaire-high-school-dropouts/

17. Article, Which One Are You?
www.worldwidelearn.com/education-articles/how-do-you-learn

18. Learning Styles.
www.chaminade.org/inspire/learnstl.htm

19. Clinebell, Howard. Understanding and Counseling Persons with Alcohol, Drug and Behavioral Addictions. (Nashville: Abingdon Press. 1984)

20. Osteen, Joel. Your Best Life Now. (New York: Faith Words, Hachette Book Group USA. 2004)

www.ingramcontent.com/pod-product-compliance
Lightning Source LLC
Chambersburg PA
CBHW020916090426
42736CB00008B/660